Bedtime Rhymes

Carol Thompson

• little • orchard •

The Man in the Moon
looked out of the moon,

Looked out of the moon and said:
'Tis time for all children on the earth
To think about going to bed!

Rub a dub dub,
Three babes in a tub
And who do you think got wet?

The daddy, the mummy,
The teddy bear's tummy,
So, hoppity, out you get!

One for
a tangle

One for
a curl

One for
a boy

One for
a girl.

One to make
a parting

One to tie
a bow

One to brush
the cobwebs out

And one to
make it grow.

Teddy bear, teddy bear
Turn around.

Teddy bear, teddy bear
Touch the ground.

Teddy bear, teddy bear
Go upstairs.
Teddy bear, teddy bear
Say your prayers.

Teddy bear, teddy bear
Turn out the light.
Teddy bear, teddy bear
Say, 'Goodnight!'

Dozily
dozily
deep in her
bed,
A little girl
dreams with the
moon in her
head.

Twinkle, twinkle, little star,
How I wonder what you are.
Up above the world so high,
Like a diamond in the sky.
Twinkle, twinkle, little star,
How I wonder what you are.